To Fly in the Sky

by Layne deMarin

Table of Contents

Consultant:
Adria F. Klein, Ph.D.
California State University, San Bernardino

capstone classroom
Heinemann Raintree • Red Brick Learning
division of Capstone

For the Birds

Long ago, people stood on the ground and watched birds flying above and wished that they could do that too. It looked like a great way to travel. People wished they could soar through the air like the birds did. They began working on flying machines.

The Chinese came up with the first flying machines hundreds of years ago by inventing kites. Kites of many colors and designs soared through the air just like birds. But humans were still stuck on the ground, just watching.

Into the Air

Then someone came up with the idea of building big wings for humans. The wings looked and flapped like bird wings, but they did not work. It seemed humans would have to come up with some other way to get off the ground.

Two brothers from France got the idea to build a different kind of flying machine. As they watched a burning fire, they saw that heat from the flames lifted small scraps of paper into the air. They used this idea to invent the **hot air balloon**.

Hot air balloons finally got people up into the air, but they could only float on the wind. It was impossible to steer a hot air balloon. So, some other inventors came up with a machine called a **glider**.

Now people could fly where they wanted to go. But there were still a few problems. For one thing, gliders often crashed. A different kind of flying machine was still needed.

The Wright Idea

Two brothers from the United States finally got it right. Wilbur and Orville Wright owned a bicycle shop. They liked building machines. They were especially interested in building a machine that could fly.

They started with a glider and then made some changes. They made it easier to steer by attaching wires to the wings. They also gave it more power by building an engine that they put on the glider.

They called their new machine the Wright Flyer. In December 1903, they tried out their new invention. It flew through the air for 12 seconds. The Wright brothers had just flown the first **airplane**.

That short flight proved that it was possible for people to fly. They started to work on building bigger, better airplanes. They figured out how to build planes that would stay in the air longer and go faster.

New Ways to Fly

The **helicopter** was designed to fly straight up off the ground. A plane can't do that. Helicopters can also fly backward. Planes can't do that either. A helicopter is very useful for rescue missions.

Jet planes have powerful engines. They can fly much faster than airplanes with propeller engines. Jet planes get people where they are going faster than ever.

A few people are flying really far and really fast. They are flying all the way into outer space on rockets. With all of these flying machines, people can finally go faster, farther, and higher than any bird ever dreamed of.

Glossary

airplane a flying machine with an engine and wings

glider a flying machine with wings and no engine

helicopter a flying machine with propellers on the top and a tail on the back

hot air balloon a flying machine with a large fabric balloon that is filled with hot air; it has a basket below for carrying passengers

propeller a set of rotating blades that give a vehicle the force it needs to move through the air or water

Index